1 HOUR a DAY to 6 FIGURES

ONE HOUR A DAY TO 6-FIGURES
How I Went From Zero To Multiple 6-Figures …and how you can too.

©2017 Steve Napolitan, Robyn Crane & Trevor Crane

All Rights Reserved. Printed in the U.S.A.

ISBN-13: 978-1544727592

ISBN-10: 1544727593

All rights reserved. This book or any portion thereof may not be reproduced or used in any manner whatsoever without the express written permission of the publisher except by a reviewer, who may quote brief passages and/or show brief video clips in a review.

Disclaimer: The Publisher and the Author make no representation or warranties with respect to the accuracy or completeness of the contents of this work and specifically disclaim all warranties of fitness for a particular purpose. No warranty may be created or extended by sales or promotional materials. The advice and strategies contained herein may not be suitable for every situation. This work is sold with the understanding that the Publisher is not engaged in rendering legal, accounting or other professional services. If professional assistance is required, the services of a competent professional person should be sought. Neither the Publisher nor the Author shall be liable for damages arising therefrom. The fact that an organization or website is referred to in this work as citation and/or potential source of further information does not mean that the Author or the Publisher endorses the information, the organization or website may provide or recommendations it may make. Further, readers should be aware that internet websites listed in this work may have changed or disappeared between when this work was written and when it is read.

Publishing and Design: Bestseller Big Business Publishing

Ordering Information: Quantity sales. Special discounts are available on quantity purchases by corporations, associations, and others. For details, contact the publisher at the address above. Orders by U.S. trade bookstores and wholesalers.

Please contact: 800-273-1625 | support@trevorcrane.com | EpicAuthor.com

First Edition

For more information about becoming a published author with Epic Author Publishing, visit: EpicAuthor.com

1 HOUR a DAY to 6 FIGURES

"How I Went From Zero To Multiple Six Figures"
...and how you can too!

#1 INTERNATIONAL BESTSELLING AUTHORS
STEVE NAPOLITAN, ROBYN CRANE & TREVOR CRANE

DEDICATION

To Jeffrey Slayter.

Your mentorship helped us create extraordinary results in record time. Without you the three of us wouldn't ever have met.

1hour6figures.com/bonus

CONTENTS

PREFACE – From Steve Napolitan xi

INTRODUCTION – Why This Book Matters 1

    ONE – What's Possible 19

    TWO – Your Future Starts Now 29

    THREE – The Stages Of The Sale 51

    FOUR – Call Your Mom 65

    FIVE – What To Say 83

    SIX – Having Fun! 95

    SEVEN – 10-Minute Calls 109

    EIGHT – Discovery Calls 129

    NINE – Strategy Sessions 145

    TEN – Do Or Die 159

HERE'S WHAT TO DO NEXT 173

ACKNOWLEDGEMENTS 175

PRODUCTS & PROGRAMS 177

ABOUT THE AUTHORS 183

PREFACE

From Steve Napolitan

I couldn't believe the nightmare I created for myself and my family.

I lost nearly everything. I say "nearly," because I still had and have my wife and three kids. *Thankfully.* But as I looked at the situation I was in, *that I had created*, I recognized how fortunate I was; because, I could have lost what is most precious to me—my family.

Luckily, my wife loved me enough, and believed in me enough, to stay with me through it all. I couldn't believe that with all my hard work, with all my best planning and good intentions, I had to start over *again*, from zero. My business had stopped. The money had stopped. We sold *all* our belongings. And, when I say all, I mean all. We didn't even have a car, or any furniture. What we had, were our clothes; and each other.

I kept asking myself, "How in the world did I get here? How could all of the blessings and opportunities I had been offered, amounted to *this*? How could it all have gone so wrong?"

Years before, I'd owned an Ad Agency that won awards, worked with fortune 100 companies and did millions in revenue. Due to our success and our phenomenal work, I started getting asked to speak and teach. I fell in love with it. I was asked to take my talents and teach other people. It was life changing.

As I grew my speaking and training business, life was good. I started getting asked to speaking all over and my family got to travel the world. Six months prior to life falling apart, I was invited to speak and train with a company in Australia, and help expand the company around the world. I took the opportunity, and I took my family with me. We sold *everything*, and gave up everything we had built in the U.S.

My family was excited and followed me and my vision, we saw it as a new, fresh, exciting time for our family.

And then the company I was working with was unable to come through with the visa they promised me. All of a sudden, I was talking to immigration lawyers and before

I knew it, we had to leave Australia, and come back to the States, where I'd abandoned everything.

The problem?

As I said, we sold everything. The business I'd built was gone. The client's I'd had, before Australia, had fallen off one by one. So there I was. I woke up, back in California, on my sister-in-laws floor. Then we got an airbnb. I'd invested, and lost, so much money on the overseas move, we had no backup savings. I had no cashflow. No speaking gigs. I felt confused, because I felt like a failure, but couldn't see how I'd dug myself into this hole.

What I did know, was that I had to build something fast, because I had to feed my family.

Now, as frustrated as I was at the time, and believe me—I was extremely upset, it turned out to be the best thing that has ever happened to me.

It turned out to be a blessing in disguise.

Sometimes, things happen in our lives that cause storms all around us. And when you first look at the storm, I'll admit, everything seems to look really, really crummy.

When I came back to America, without a way of feeding my family. I needed something fast. I was willing to work hard, but I also wasn't willing to give *all* of my time, to building things back. Having learned this lesson the hard way, in the past, I refused to sacrifice time, and the most important thing to me in the world—*my wife and kids*.

I didn't have time to mess around. So I didn't.

I didn't waste time on things that wouldn't create results. I cut off all other distractions, and all other non-money making activities. I had to focus.

First, I had to choose what business I wanted to be in. Second, I took action.

And that's it.

You see, I had already seen what this power of focus could mean for me and my business, so I cut out all of the "extra" non-essentials, and I took action.

The result?

Within 90 days I created over $250,000 in revenue and ultimately got myself back on my feet, and where I needed to be.

That is what this book is about.

I want to teach you what I did in 90 days to book over $250,000 in revenue and ultimately build what is now making me over $100,000 a month.

But I didn't choose to write this book alone, and only give you one perspective. Instead, you'll get three.

This book was born from a conversation I had with two friends, Robyn and Trevor Crane. After traveling across the country to speak at a conference, I chose to stay a couple of extra days at their house. As we talked about our businesses, we considered what we might create together, that would offer the BIGGEST benefit to our clients.

What we discovered, was that each of us used a very similar process to grow our businesses. Yes, they are a married couple now, but they both used this strategy, independently; to grow 6-Figures and beyond.

So we put our heads together, and created a simple step-by-step system that we each have used to generate revenue and rapid results.

Thus, *One Hour A Day To 6-Figures*, was born.

The best thing is, it's simple. And it works. I like simple. And I only like to share what works. YOU WILL NOT FIND A BUNCH OF CRAP TO WASTE YOUR TIME IN THIS BOOK.

Instead, you'll find exactly what you need, to transform your life and your business. This book is short and to the point.

Simplicity is *key* to your success.

In this book, we're going to ask you to do three things:

1. Keep it simple.
2. Commit to one hour a day.
3. Get help.

This simple discipline and activity that we'll share with you in this book, can change your life, as it has ours.

So here we go.

We are so excited to share with you exactly how to work your business. We've broken it down, as if we were working with you PERSONALLY… to help you implement this quickly, and start seeing results.

It's a simple, yet powerful way to invest just ONE hour per day.

There's no need to over-complicate this.

If you read this book and follow what we say you will be able to have amazing results in just one hour a day.

Now, just to be clear, you will still need to spend more time than an hour to run your business. Yes you will need to spend time having sales meetings, and you'll need to spend time fulfilling your promises to clients, and doing bookkeeping, etc. Unless you hire someone. Either way, it still has to be done.

What we're saying is, you will need to adjust your behavior to allow time for, strike that, to CREATE THE DISCIPLINE of investing just, ONE HOUR A DAY, (five days a week) to this system.

The result will be new leads for your business.

No, you do not need to invest in spending-money on marketing. (At least, at this stage.)

Instead, you will learn, how in just one hour a day you can book the meetings you need with the right clients, to jump-start your revenue.

This will allow you to STOP wasting loads of time on things that aren't creating results… Instead, we want you to start closing more deals—NOW.

So when you read this book, note that you will be getting the best of all three authors of this book. Consider this to be a personal, private consultation with each of us.

In fact, we'll keep it in a conversational format, that will make this a quick read, but utterly impactful.

Are you ready? We hope you are.

Let's do this.

-Steve

INTRODUCTION

"The only limit to your impact is your imagination and commitment."
—Tony Robbins

Welcome to One Hour A Day to 6-Figures!

ROBYN:

We are excited to share this with you, because we believe it is the simplest and fastest way to create a client on-demand system. (We'll describe more about what that means throughout this book.)

I'm Robyn Crane, and I'd like to also introduce you to, my husband Trevor Crane and Steve Napolitan.

We are so grateful to share these insights with you, here inside of this book.

TREVOR:

Hello! Trevor here! (*Imagine me waving at you through these pages…*)

STEVE:

And I'm Steve Napolitan! (*I'm waving as well.*)

TREVOR:

As the title of this book suggests, we're going to show you a simple discipline that you can use to generate 6-Figures PLUS… all without spending any money on marketing.

Anyone can apply this, (yes anyone) as long as you're willing to follow this process.

Also, as Robyn just mentioned, we will be referring to this as a "client on demand" system throughout this book. We do that for a reason.

Let me ask you a question:

When you want water to come out of a faucet in your house, what do you do?

You turn the knob right?

And what happens? Water comes out.

Well imagine, what it would be like if every time you wanted another "amazing" client, you just turned on your "client on demand" system, and you got all the clients you wanted?

Would that be cool?

Because that's what you're going to be getting with this book.

"If" you commit to the discipline of just one hour a day, five days a week, and you're "willing" to take action.

STEVE:

Yep, Trevor's right. I couldn't have said it better… we speak from experience, because it's happened for each of us… with just one hour a day.

TREVOR:

We'll show you what to do. And, we'll show you what not to do.

And the best thing is, we've made this simple.

And please believe us, when we tell you that this subject is very personal to each of us… Using what we'll show you in this book, helped me build my life back after I filed a $2.2 Million Dollar bankruptcy.

I'm not proud of it, but at one point, I found myself homeless.

I felt so hopeless, at one point, that I couldn't see a way out of the debt and despair, and began to doubt every single move I made.

This system brought me back.

Today, I have nearly everything I've wanted.

Today, I get to travel the world and spend my days transforming lives.

Today, I'm married to the most beautiful woman in the world, and I have the most amazing daughter in the world.

Today, I only do things that are important to me. (And those priorities have shifted, my friend.)

Today, instead of working so hard—to the point of destroying nearly all of my personal and professional relationships, as I did in the past—my time is focused more effectively.

Today, I don't have to work as many hours, so I can focus my attention on the connection I have with my 9-year old daughter and the rest of my family.

Today, I get to earn a fortune, without killing and sacrificing the quality time I get to spend with my family. We get to spend time together doing what we love to do most.

It's difficult for me to describe how transformational and positive this discipline has affected my life. But I'm not going to get into my story too much here.

What we are so grateful for, is to be able to share this simple discipline with you. And, better for you we're writing this book in an extremely fun and entertaining way, so you can hear each of our voices, and our experiences using this system.

STEVE:

Thanks for sharing that Trevor, and the same goes for me.

Before I started using this system, I was working way too hard for way too little.

But when I created the habit of one hour a day to create this client on-demand system, it changed my life and my family's.

Within 90 days, I was generating multiple six-figures in income.

ROBYN:

For most people, their biggest problem is getting leads. Often times, the gap seems to be, "How do I attract the right clients?" And, "How can I consistently get high-paying, amazing clients in my business."

This book, and this system solves this problem.

Like Trevor said, what we really want to do here is help you have a client on-demand system. We want to help you get them right away. We're talking the right clients. The ones that you want to work with. The ones who can't wait to work with you as well.

This way, your business can have consistent income. And you can experience the freedom and the peace of mind that comes from knowing you have a system that works.

Trevor even wore a shirt with wings on it today, to remind you that you can fly. You can fly!

TREVOR:

"I believe I can fly!" (Trevor singing)

STEVE:

That's good. (Steve laughs)

Most Businesses Suffer With These Problems:

- Being busy, but not productive at generating leads, sales and revenue.

- Not earning the money they want.

- Struggling to grow their business and add the right clients. (leads, and sales)

- Gambling with their marketing, like it's a slot machine, putting money in, and not knowing what to expect.

- They don't know "WHY." Not knowing why things work in their business when they do work, or why things aren't working when they don't.

ROBYN:

But truly, if you are reading this now and you're struggling to create consistent income, then what you are holding in your hands is exactly what you and your business need.

This can set you up to take off and create exactly what you want in your business and your life.

STEVE:

And I just want to second all of that, and add something else. Most people think that sometimes it's hard to get clients. Or that it's up to chance.

They tell themselves, "Maybe this month I'm going to have clients." Or, "Maybe next month I'm not."

Then quickly thereafter they think, "Oh NO! What am I going to do?! Ahhhhh!!!"

With this system we share with you inside of these pages, we know, beyond a shadow of a doubt, that you will be able to turn the "faucet" and begin to turn your income off and on, at will.

If you think, "You know, I think I want some more clients." Then, that's okay… turn it up a little bit. If you want less, you might think, "I want less, let's turn it back down."

You will literally be able to do that. I've done it personally. Robyn and Trevor have done it. Now you'll be able to do it as well.

So we're ready to give you everything that we can in this book. And I want to tell you right now, we are doing everything in our power to not just set that intention, but do deliver it too.

We've talked about it. The three of us are committed.

We're going to give you everything we can, from the bottom of our hearts so that you can take this into your business, and create results now.

We just need one thing from you:

We need you to commit, to you.

Not to us. Because we're doing just fine. We're good.

We're using this already and it works.

But we want it to work for you.

And we can't do it alone. This has to be teamwork.

It's like we are giving you gold in these pages.

ROBYN:

Steve, we ARE going to give them gold! (Cheering)

STEVE:

That's it! But here's the thing… you have to take it and do something with it.

Otherwise, it's worth nothing.

Otherwise, you should just put this book down right now and go do something else. You can go sit on your couch and dream about having more income.

And you might think, "Oh, Steve's being a little harsh right now" but I am saying this because I made a personal commitment. And I'm doing this with Robyn and Trevor because they have the same commitment that I have.

We want to make a difference in your life.

And the only way that's going to happen is if you commit to doing this.

And we're going to ask that you play full out.

Take all the notes you can, and then you need to take this and implement it into your business—so you can have the results you want.

TREVOR:

That's right. We're going to give you the exact action plan that each of us have used, and would use if we were to start over, right now from scratch.

Plus, we're going to have a lot of fun together because we want this whole process to be cool for you!

STEVE:

You have to have fun.

I mean, you have to be *willing* to have fun.

ALL:

(Laughs)

STEVE:

Because we like to have fun.

ROBYN:

We do.

TREVOR:

I've also got to add something.

You're going to get a few different perspectives here in this book, because the three of us are going to tag team this.

You're going to hear from Robyn, Steve and me. All three of us are going to take turns, going back and forth.

We've also broken this down into nice simple chapters, so it makes it easy for you to digest.

We're going to show you exactly what to say, how to spend your time, the exact action plan so you know exactly what you've got to go do.

And Like Steve said, it's important that you commit to this, because we're here and ready to help you.

Is there anything else we need to cover guys?

ROBYN:

I just want to say you've definitely come to the right place.

There's a lot of BS out there… and a bunch of people who are only willing to give you "fluff." This is not fluff.

This is the real deal.

What we will give you right now is really going to help you, and as we keep saying, your job is to apply it.

Now if you catch yourself looking at this and thinking, "Oh duh! Obviously, if you're willing to do that, and you're willing to work hard, then of course you can make six figures… but I don't really want to do that."

Then kick yourself in the ass.

Sure, that's your choice. But, then you're settling for so much less than you can be. We believe in you, and we know you can do this.

We're going to give you the exact things that you need, so you can apply them right away and really get the results you want, and the results you need.

That means cash on-demand.

That means it's also your dreams-on-demand.

Plus, if you have any questions, just reach out to us. We're here for you.

We're going to all add our personal contact information, and websites, and social media links in this book, so you can reach out to us for help if you need it.

Or you can just celebrate with us.

WE'D LOVE TO HEAR THAT!

STEVE:

So that's it.

If you want to, just reach out to any one of us, and we can point you in the right direction.

TREVOR:

Alright let's move on to the first chapter!

The Key Benefits of This Book

- Simple way to earn more money, and create more clients on demand… stress-free.

- Simple habit to find the right person to talk to, and the ideal customer you want to work with.

- Simple, streamlined, repeatable, "anyone can do it" system to grow their business to six-figures (or more). Time commitment? One-hour a day.

- Know what you are doing that you shouldn't be doing. And finally know what you should be doing, that you aren't doing yet.

Key Takeaways

- Most people struggle doing activities that aren't money-producing. They are busy, but not productive at generating leads, sales, and revenue.

- The first secret sauce behind all success, is commitment. Interested means you'll only do what's convenient. Being committed means you'll do whatever it takes.

- The one hour a day to six figures system, shows you how you can get clients on demand. Using this system, you will be able to add an extra six figures to your current income, and have the power to increase your income at will.

CHAPTER

ONE

ONE
What's Possible

*"We make a living by what we get.
We make a life by what we give."*
—Winston Churchill

TREVOR:

Here's a question for you, and I'll ask you to think very carefully about your answer.

"How many clients do you wish you could get 'rid of' and you're just working with for the money? "

These are clients you wouldn't consider your ideal or perfect clients, but ones that you tolerate.

One of the main strengths of this strategy is to help you pick the best people to work with. We want you to have so many leads, of your perfect, or what Steve likes to call your Wow Client, that you shift your activity and behavior to doing only those things that you enjoy, and that you finally start earning the money you desire.

How cool would it be to, "Close more deals in less time? And only talk to the types of people you want to work with?"

ROBYN:

I'd like to add something here.

Because what is most important to me is to help more people.

You're likely here because you want more clients, and also because you want more money in your pocket. But I'm going to guess that you want even more than that.

I really believe that the more money you make is representative of the value you provide and number of people you help.

What I want for you is, yes, you get more clients. Yes, you'll get more cash in your pockets. But I believe, that the way you do this is by making a bigger impact and helping more people.

I believe that "sales" equals "helping people."

When you help more people, you make more money.

TREVOR:

Spot on Robyn. I'd also like to emphasize how important it is to get clear about the reasons for doing this... also called your "WHY."

Yes, the money is important. But making money isn't the end goal. It's about "impact" like Robyn said.

Believe it or not, one of the fastest ways for you to create bigger, better results is to get clear on your WHY, that is the mission that's greater than yourself.

The bigger your why, the bigger your bank account.

So, I have a few questions for you. (Not Robyn.) You, the reader.

I'd like you to take a moment to consider, "What would it mean to you if you looked forward to every-single call, or interaction, you had with your client?

What would it be like, if you could woke up every morning, excited to serve them?

What if you could choose exactly "how many" clients you wanted to work with, and earn "precisely" the amount of money you wanted to earn?

Better yet, what if every day you worked in your business, felt like an chance for you to fill-in the amount of a blank check?

Take a few moments now to consider what you really want and why.

"It's hard to get where you want to go, if you don't know where you are going." —Trevor Crane

EXERCISE

Use this space to answer these questions.

Your Current #'s?

1. How many _____ are you getting every _____?

2. How many _____ are you getting every _____?

3. How many _____ do you _____ every month?

Key Takeaways

- Work with people you enjoy working with. It makes earning money fun! You must change your mindset from just settling for what you get, to getting what you want.

- Making more money is all about impact. You go into business to make a difference. The bigger your why, the bigger your reason for being of service to something greater than yourself, the bigger your bank account.

- Selling and making more money is about helping more people, and giving them the opportunity to transform their lives. When you are making more money, it is a demonstration that you are adding more value to people's lives.

CHAPTER

TWO

TWO
Your Future Starts Now

"A goal properly set is halfway reached."
—Abraham Lincoln

ROBYN:

Okay, this chapter is all about you and your goals.

You've got to keep your eye on the prize. First, you want to know what you want so that you can go after it and get it!

I work with a lot of financial planners and one of their biggest problems is actually getting consistent leads come into their practice.

Part of the problem is they say they don't have time. They're so busy serving existing clients, they don't have enough time to go out and generate more leads.

Steve's going to share something with you soon, about how you can use a small amount of time and get a huge, huge result.

To give you an example of the POWER of this, Jessica, a financial advisor and client of mine, used this system to make $3600 in only 2 days!

What I typically ask my clients is, "Okay, how many leads are you actually getting, let's say each week in your business?"

I want you to think of the same thing because it's important to know where you're starting right now. This way, we can discover the path to get you from there, to where you want to go. (Our goal is to help you get there, right? Awesome!)

Like using any map, you have to get clear on Point A before you know how to get to Point B. Exercise – Where Are You Now?

EXERCISE

How many leads are you getting each week? (Write it down.)

_____

_____

_____

If that's every week consistently, you can multiply it by four to know how many leads you're getting in a month.

Now I say, "getting" as if getting more leads just magically happens. But obviously, you've got to go do something to get leads coming in.

Before they started working with me, some of my clients say they're getting one, two, maybe five new leads a month. When I hear an answer like this, I know right away why their business isn't growing the way they want it to.

Now I want you to write down how many do you want to get per week, or even each month?

If you're only getting five leads per month, do you want twenty-five per month? Do you want fifty?

What difference would it make in your business if you had five times or ten times the amount of "qualified" leads coming into your business?

Think about that for a moment, and write it down.

EXERCISE

Setting the Goal for Number of Leads

How many leads do you want to get each week? (Write it down.)

_____

_____

_____

_____

Next, I want you to write down how much money are you making now, each month. Just write down an average.

People often say, "Oh, well, sometimes it's this and that etc." Don't worry about it. Just get an average.

EXERCISE

How Much Are You Earning Now?

How much money are you earning on average now, per month? (Write it down.)

_____
_____
_____
_____

If you don't know these numbers, by the way, that's okay for now, but…

That's a problem.

You need to know your numbers and track your numbers because you want **results**.

What gets measured gets done.

Write down how much money you're making.

Then, of course, you're going to write down how much do you want to make.

Don't think about what's possible and don't think about whether it's going to be able to work for you.

Right now, I just want you to dream. Pretend you're waving a magic wand…

Write down what you want because, **you can make anything happen**.

EXERCISE

How Much Money Would You Like to Be Earning?

If you could wave a magic wand, how much money would you be earning on average now, per month?

_____

_____

_____

_____

Now that you have those numbers, I'm going to bring in Steve. He's going to show you the real magical stuff. How would you like to know about how you could trade just a little bit of your time, to create an extraordinarily huge result?

Well, here you go then... Tag team!

STEVE:

Tagged, I'm in! (High five)

Robyn just set the tone for what you want.

Whatever it is for you, you want to be able to make those deals. Now we want to talk about how we get more leads and how do we get it on demand.

To explain what I want to share, I'm going to start with a number: 1,440.

For just a moment, let's say that you added this number of qualified leads to your business.

What if you talked to 1,440 people who might want to hire you? Do you think that would make an impact in your business? I think so.

Yes, that's quite a number of leads.

Now, you might think it's a big number; maybe it sounds overwhelming. But what if I said, that 1,440 leads was the number of leads you get over the course of a year?

Well that's just 120 per month. That's a little easier to think about starting with? Sound better?

If we want to reach 1,440 leads in a year, we need to talk to 120 people per month.

Is that still a big number? It may be for you, maybe 120 is still a big number. Let's break it down further now, to what that would mean in a week.

If we divide 120 by 4, we get 30 leads per week. So in order to gain 1,440 leads per year, all you would have to talk to is 30 leads per week. (I know this is approximate, since some months have five weeks. Dividing by 4 gets you pretty close and on those months with 5 weeks, guess what, you get even more leads.)

Now, you may be thinking in your head "that's still a lot."

You're like, "Steve, that's adding 30 new people that I have to reach out to? Where am I going to find them? And, how am I going to handle that?"

If you're asking those questions, we'll get there. Keep reading.

Let's take this a step even further.

Let's say you work 5 days a week. Let's divide 30 by 5. Now, that's just 6 leads per day.

Now is that number a little bit more reasonable? I think so. What I have found, is that 6 leads a day, seems a lot more digestible.

The same principle applies for all goals. When we're talking about goals, I want you to think about looking at your goals in a new way.

Consider one of your big yearly goals. Then, chunk it down to what needs to happen every month, then you chunk it down to a week, then you chunk it down to a day.

If I reach out to six people a day, that will get me 30 per week, that's going to get me 120 per month, and that's going to get me 1,440 per year.

Now let me tell you something that few people would believe… By me just committing to getting six leads per day, I changed my life!

If I came to you and I said I have this amazing pizza. It's the best pizza ever! Is it possible that you might want a slice just to taste it?

But if I was like, "No, you cant! Instead, I want you to eat the whole thing!"

And then, I shoved the whole pizza in your mouth. At that point, you probably won't be worried about the taste of the pizza. You'd just trying to breathe and not choke to death!

That's the same thing that can happen when you first try to grasp the idea of 1,400 plus people in your mind. It's way too big.

But that's why we chunk it down.

You might even be thinking, "Steve, you're talking about so much work. You mean, I have to talk to that many people?"

Here's a story I want you to think for a moment. It's about "FARMING."

Most business owners are sitting on their land, on their dirt, and waiting for a bird to fly in and drop a seed, "Oh, there's a bird! It's coming!"

Then what? The seed drops on your land. You then grab a bucket of water, run over, and start watering it. You take care of it. You make sure the tree is getting everything it needs, and you get to collect the yield.

Problem is, you are only relying on that one tree, and you have to wait for new birds who happen to fly buy and drop seeds on your property.

You can probably imagine, that that strategy might only yield so much income, or in this case, a very limited "harvest."

Imagine, that the farmer only had that one client, or that one tree. And then they just sat around and waiting for another bird to come by, hoping they'd drop another seed. Then they think, "Shoot! It's been three weeks and I haven't got a bird. That sucks!"

Is that happening for you?

I'll tell you right now, in business if you're not farming, if you're not running your farm, then you might as well not have it.

What if Trevor, Robyn, and I owned land, a big farm, and we choose to plant a crop?

We would find the seeds, and plant them ourselves. Then water them, and care for them, so we benefit from the yield. And the more we plant, the more yield we can have.

We don't leave it to chance. We commit to it by choice.

Can you imagine if we went and bought 100 acres and we did nothing with it and just let it sit there? That's not going to serve us. We would have to pay for that farm every month without making any return on it.

I'm telling you right now, you have to plant seeds. You have to farm.

What I want to do is make it really easy for you. I want you to do a little bit each day. Plant six seeds per day. And we are going to show you how to make reaching out to six leads a day simple.

So, I'm not telling you to go plant 1,440 seeds today like a farmer would. They'd bring in a big, old tractor and do that. They'd invest in their business, with a bunch of tools and external resources.

That's not you. Not yet. For now, you're just going to do six seeds a day. And if, and when, you do that consistently, you're going to have big yields!

You can SCALE your business, and really excel things once you've mastered the basics. (I CANNOT STRESS THIS ENOUGH.)

For now, keep it simple.

I like simple.

Why?

Simple works.

Like Trevor said, you're going to be able to "pick" how many clients you want to work with, and earn the money you want.

EXERCISE

Committing to One Hour a Day of Calls

How much money do you want to make?

_____

How much money does one client make you?

_____

How many leads does it take for you to convert one into a client?

_____

How many leads do you need to generate to earn the money you want?

_____

How many people are you going to commit to talking to a day?

_____

Now let me break this down quickly, to show you how easily you can do this.

Let's say you want to start out with making three calls a day. You do it every day. Let's even say you were going to start with one a day, just for right now, that's five leads. That means you'll have 20 leads a month.

Now if it were me, and just one of those leads converted to a private paying client, that's worth at least $75,000 to me! Each private coaching client I have brings in about $75,000-$100,000 per year.

And I can tell you now from experience, the fastest, quickest, and least effort is when I make phone calls. I've found they get me the quickest response.

You might be saying, "Oh, that's what this is about? This is about making phone calls or reaching out to people?" Yes, it is. Yes, it is.

If you want leads on demand, it starts with making the calls. Yes you can do Facebook or Email, or text, sure. I have experience using those forms of marketing too. I do that too.

But I'm telling you now, the fastest way to get into action, gain leads, and get more clients by demand, is making calls.

If you don't believe me, you can try making a week of calls and then the next week do email. Track what happens and see which one provides more leads. Keep doing what works.

All you need to do, is set one hour a day to make those calls. If it is six calls, that are 10 mins per call, that is 60 minutes.

Trevor: Okay I'm going to tap in. Literally, Steve and I were just hanging out and having some fun. We asked the question about what would give YOU the best possible thing, that would help you create the fastest results.

We also asked the question of what has helped "us" get the most clients, and make the most money, and have the most impact in our own lives.

For both of us, it came down to the same thing. This.

It's what Steve is showing you right now.

We both committed to this simple discipline.

For you, we're talking about YOU now getting clients on demand, with only investing one hour a day.

One hour a day where you're setting appointments and getting leads.

That's it.

Let's get back to the gift, or the benefit of this discipline.

That gift of just having this discipline has made me, all of my clients, and my wife, Robyn—multiple six figures in additional income.

I teach my personal one-to-one high paying clients the same. I get them to pick up the phone, to reach out, and contact people for simple 10-minute calls. You may already be asking, "What do you mean by a 10-minute call?"

We will share that with you soon. Don't worry, it's in this book. We are going to give you all the steps.

If you struggle keeping yourself accountable like many of my private clients did, then Steve, Robyn and I each have mentoring programs that you can enroll for personalized help.

Just reach out. We are here to help you.

I promise you, once you start getting results, you'll wake-up looking forward to making those calls. I guarantee it.

So I think that's about it for this chapter.

In the next chapter, Robyn's going to share with you the details of what we call the, Stages of the Sale, and where this actually fits in to your business, so that you can start getting those clients.

Your Current $?

1. How much _____ are you making now? Per _____?

2. How much _____ are you making now? Per _____?

3. How much _____ do you _____ to make every month?

Key Takeaways

- You must get real with where you are now, before writing down where you want to be. Point B on the map is useless if you don't know your Point A.

- No goal is realistic until you chunk it down. If you don't chunk it down, you will experience overwhelm, and you won't take action. A confused mind does nothing. So whatever goal you set for your year, break it down into measurable actions; monthly, weekly, daily, and even down to the hour.

- Business is like farming. You have to plant seeds, consistently water them, and care for the crop. You don't wait for things to happen. You take the right daily actions to make it happen.

- The fastest way to get more leads, is to pick up the phone. You will be shown what to say in the coming chapters of the book. But just remember, picking up the phone doesn't have to be daunting. Once you chunk it down, it can be done by making 6 or less 10-minute calls per day. How many calls you make all depends on your goal of how much money you want to earn.

CHAPTER

THREE

THREE
The Stages of The Sale

*"Great things are not done by impulse,
but by a series of small things brought together."*
—Vincent Van Gogh

ROBYN:

Welcome to Chapter 3, the Stages of the Sale!

This is assuming you're committed to making your calls. We will help make this simple for you.

As Steve has said, and Trevor and I agree—making the calls is one of the fastest ways to get a steady stream of clients now. Of course, you can do other activities—*that's your choice*—but you've got to do something actively, daily that makes those connections.

Now you might be wondering, *"Okay. What do I do now? I'm going to make some calls. But, I don't know <u>what</u> to say. I don't know <u>who</u> to call."*

We're going to cover all that soon. So don't worry.

But first things first. You have to know the stages of the sale. You have to know the steps you're taking people through, so you know what's coming up—*like a roadmap*.

What a lot of people have problems with, and what they make mistakes doing, is that they don't even know *where* they're driving people to.

In fact, I did this the other day. We do this all the time, we still make mistakes. It's great, because we learn it for you so you don't have to do it.

I was literally on the phone the other day. I met someone at a financial planning meeting, an FPA meeting for women.

At the meeting, I met this woman who was great, and we connected, and I thought "Okay, I'm going to follow up!"

I sent her an email, I followed up, and we set an appointment on the calendar. Yay!

Initially I thought, *"Ok, great. I'm just going to connect with this woman."* My intention was not to sell her or make her a client.

I was just going to connect. So I got on the phone, I wasn't totally clear about what the next step was, and as I was talking to her I realized, *"Oh, wait, she could be this great client. She would be perfect for my program."*

I totally started to change my focus and started talking about her problems and then tried to drive her to something else that I wasn't planning on doing.

I totally screwed up the connection call, and by the end I totally felt like she was feeling sold to. And she did, which was not my intention.

I just thought, *"Oh my gosh, I can really help this woman."* I'm very passionate about that. But I completely screwed it up and I could feel the energy change.

Why did it happen? Because I wasn't clear about the stage of the sale. I wasn't clear about the next step of what I was driving her to. Instead, I tried to *drive* her to some program.

Here's all you have to consider, when it comes to the "sales process:"

"Sales" is simply just about driving people to the next step.

Now, let me show you how this works.

The first step, if you're going from, let's say, a networking event—the first step you want to move people to after that is to schedule a "Connection call."

Let's just assume it's kind of a cold-ish or warm lead. You're going to start with a connection call.

The purpose of this call is to, you guessed it: to connect.

Hey, isn't that awesome? All you need to do is connect. We named it connection call for a reason.

Remember, the main purpose of this call is to drive them to the next step. It's not to *sell* them, it's not to have them *become a client*, nothing else.

Only to drive them to the next step.

So what's the next step? The next step is a ten-minute call. This is what Steve was talking about, your ten-minute calls.

Now when you first start this process, and you're like, "Okay, I'm going to start, Monday morning is going to be my very first time to make my six calls, that's awesome."

It's going to be a little easier at first because all you have to do is make a quick connection.

This connection call could be two minutes. It doesn't have to be ten minutes. So you can make even more than 6 calls if you want.

Next, you're going to get them on your calendar for a ten minute call. That's the next step!

Okay, you don't know what to say yet, you're not sure what you do, you don't know who to call. Don't worry. We're going to cover that too. I'm just going through the *stages* of the sale. So you have a system. So you understand the process.

So, first step? Connection call.

Next step? Ten-minute call.

Recently, I met a woman at a networking event. After we met, I simply made a quick call to her, connected for two brief minutes, just to find out if she was "curious" about getting help with her business.

I could have easily tried to have a ten minute call with her, but instead I kept it short and sweet. I was only interested to know if she was even *curious* about getting my help.

If I had pushed her, she might have felt like I was trying to *convince* her to work with me.

But instead, I set another appointment for our ten-minute call.

During that call, I'll find out if they want a *discovery call*.

The purpose, is to know the outcome for each step.

The first outcome from the connection call is to drive them to the next step, the ten-minute call. Then the discovery call, etc.

QUICK NOTE HERE:

Now, before we talk about the discovery call, we want you to know the 1 hour a day that we are talking about is for the connection calls and the 10-minute calls.

As Steve said 6 – 10-minute calls = 1 hour.

The time you spend on your Discovery Calls and your Strategy Sessions are meetings you already do (or should have been doing.) Those will take extra time.

What you are doing right now, is meeting with people or leads, hoping they are a fit. The 1 hour a day system, is using the connecting call and the 10-minute call, so that you can increase your leads every day.

If you do this daily, connecting to 6 people 5 times a week, that will total 1,440 a year. This also saves you hours and hours of not having to have longer meetings with people that are not a fit.

With the first connection, most of us spend 30 minutes or more. These people may not be a good fit to work with us or buy our product. This will add up to 3-6 hours a day or more, for the same volume of connections. When really we should start with much less time. Then only give the longer meetings to those that maybe a good fit.

The Discovery Call and the Strategy Session (we'll explain those next) are longer meetings that you only do with the right leads. These meetings can replace the sales meetings you may be doing now and does not count toward the 1 hour a day.

During the discovery call, you'll ask some questions to find out if they're *really* a prospect for you, not just a lead. A prospect is someone who has the potential to work with you, and is actually someone you would LOVE to work with!

Remember what Trevor said in Chapter 1? It's about working with clients you want, and getting paid what you want.

Now, all these calls are FREE calls. It could be different for everybody's business. But in general, You don't charge money for it.

From the discovery call, you're going to drive them to the *strategy session*. This is a paid session. That's right, you start getting paid!

Paid for your time to have a real sales conversation, so we can help them have transformation in their life. That means you get paid to have sales conversations! Pretty awesome.

We talk about this in more depth in Chapter 9. But here's the result: Your Strategy Session, and the entire sales process becomes incredibly valuable to the client all on it's own. Regardless of if the client "buys" from you or not, the result is that you have served your prospect.

Again, the purpose of the *strategy session*, even though it is paid, is to then drive them to the next step. You share your expertise, you add a ton of value, and you drive them to the next step of becoming a client.

"If" you discover it is a match. "If" you can see yourself working with them. "If" you'd love working with them. Then, you're going to offer your products or services and close the deal.

Not just any client. A client you love. A client you get to select.

The fact that you take these extra steps, BEFORE you spend the time to do a strategy session, saves you time.

It also allows you to make deeper connections, and to add and establish "value" during every stage of the sales process.

This way, your prospect feels comfortable with you, and no matter what happens, whether they work with you or not, they leave with a great experience.

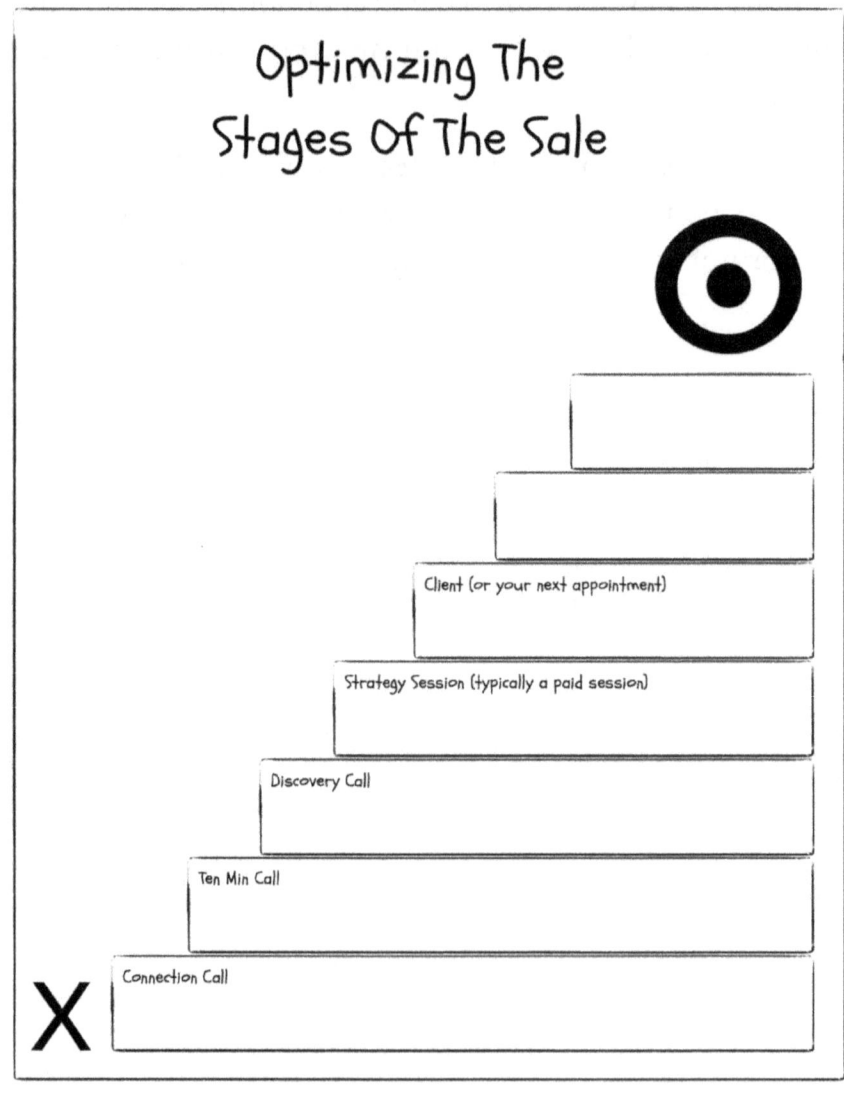

Key Takeaways

- Most people spend time calling someone they thought would be a good client, only ending up with the person; not signing up, or walking away because they felt pushed.

- So you speak to someone at a networking event, exchange business cards… now what? Most people don't know this answer. Without knowing where you are driving your prospects to, you end up spending time thinking you are generating leads… but you aren't.

- Understanding stages of the sale is about understanding where you are driving your prospect to next. You must know what the next step is. The stages of sale are; connection call, ten-minute call, discovery call, strategy session (paid), and then finally, closing the deal (if they are a good fit) and having a paying client.

CHAPTER

FOUR

FOUR
Call Your Mom

"Networking is marketing. Marketing yourself, marketing your uniqueness, marketing what you stand for."
—Christine Comaford-Lynch

TREVOR:

Welcome to Chapter 4. We're going to talk about what you're really doing here in your business, which is setting appointments, and who you're going to call. That reminds me of Ghostbusters. ***"Who ya ganna call?"***

Let's get right down to it. This whole process and even your business - any business - can be broken down into two parts:

Setting appointments.

Keeping appointments.

The stages of the sale that Robyn just shared tell you what steps you are driving someone to. For example, if you meet someone at a conference, you set the first appointment.

If you meet someone that you think may be a good fit to work with, you ask them, "Hey, let's set-up a quick call?" Then you move them to the connection call, discovery call, and so forth.

You just want to make sure you're setting appointments. But you've got to have the discipline of following through and actually keeping the appointments. You've got to make sure you have that discipline.

Like Steve said at the very beginning of this, we're hoping you have committed 100% to playing full out and commit to your own business. Don't commit to us. Commit to you. This is for you. One hour a day of setting appointments and having short calls with people.

Let's be totally clear about what we're talking about: the time you're spending in this one hour, is about setting the appointments.

Robyn mentioned that first call is only going to be one to two minutes. You're there for one purpose and one purpose only, to go to the next step. Which is the ten-minute call. Or NOT.

If it is *not* the right fit, you move on and that saves you time.

Every step, moving forward cost more time. During each step you are deciding if they are a fit for your service or product, or not. If you discover it's not a fit during the connection call or the 10-minute call—*you are saving tons of time.*

If you get to the discovery call and it is not the right fit, it's still less than the strategy session. And even if you get to the strategy session and it's not a fit it will still save you so much time from having the wrong client.

Having a client become a customer service headache, is NOT your goal.

In short, I'm saying work with the right people and the quicker you figure that out, the more *time* and *happiness* you gain in your life.

Now, back to booking calls.

How can you do that? We've been talking a lot about the phone because it's such an awesome way to build rapport.

It's such an amazing way to set the appointment, but let's face it, there's a couple of other ways you can do it. Steve mentioned this that he's used different methods such as Facebook messages.

So if during this one hour a day that, you're actually in activity where you're trying to set these appointments on Facebook, it's okay for you to send Facebook messages.

It's okay for you to have an email that you send out.

But here's what I want to talk about. This is key.

This is NOT an hour spent where you're writing the email. That's not it. This is not where you're crafting all of it.

This isn't where you go find your list of who you're going to talk to (I'm going to talk about that later in this chapter), you're going to pick up the phone, and it is game on. You're going to have a timer and your job is to set appointments.

If you want to pick up the phone, if you want to text message someone… you choose. Just stick with one. You can also used LinkedIn, you could use Snapchat.

Use whatever vehicle you want to set the appointment.

For example:

If I use text message at a speaking or networking event, I'll text the person my number, I'll give them my name right away, and sometimes I'll try to set that connection appointment immediately on the spot.

Here's what's cool. If you want, reach out to us, and we'll give you some template texts to use and customize. You can message us, and request this through this link: <u>1hour6figures.com</u>

You would then want to customize those messages on *your* time. This is not about using your hour a day to start writing and doing all the copywriting for the script. That's not it.

This is not time that you're going to talk to them about the football game last night. This is not the time you're going to talk about the Walking Dead. This is not time that you're going to get into anything else.

Now, the next question is WHO do you call? A lot of people think, "Oh my God. I don't know…"

You probably have a shoebox full of business cards at home. You probably have some people in your phone. I think Steve was telling me, and he can go ahead and address this because he's going to be here in just a second, how many average phone numbers people keep in their cell phones. It's something like 200, 300, 600, or so.

When I wrote my book, *<u>High Paying Clients</u>*, I did some research and it says that the average person knows 600 people. 600 people that you can put on your list.

How many people are you connected with on LinkedIn or Twitter or Facebook?

What you're going to need when you are setting these appointments is a list of people to call.

I'm going to go ahead and turn a little bit of this over to Steve Napolitan to share some magic with you.

STEVE:

Here I am!

TREVOR:

Tag! (*Trevor smiles and let's Steve take over…*)

STEVE:

I'm going to tell you a little bit about who to call and I wanted to start with a little issue that I had many years ago.

Many years ago in my business I was struggling. I remember I used to have my desk and I faced this board. I had this white board and I put my leads on the board.

I remember one day sitting at the board and I was like, *"Man, if that lead only did this, and if that lead did this, and if that lead did this, I would have business."*

I was basically stuck complaining about how difficult the leads were, and if only they changed, it would make my life easier.

I was so frustrated I didn't know what to do. So I called this one guy I knew that had done really well in business. He wasn't necessarily like an ongoing coach, but it was someone that I looked to for some advice.

I called him and said, "Hey, this is Steve. I need to talk to you about my business right now." I tell him something along the lines of, "This lead is doing that, this lead's doing this, etc." It was all about what the leads were doing with their lives.

Then he stopped me. He said, "Steve, Stop!" I respond, "Yeah, what's up?" He said, "You're blaming the leads." I said, "Yeah, I guess I am. I'm blaming the leads. You got me."

He said, "Well, what can you do about it?" I said, "Well I guess I can get new leads," and he said, "Perfect. Do that." I said, "I guess I could use a little help there. I don't know where to get more leads. That's why I think I'm focusing on these leads that I do have because I don't know where to get more leads."

Then he said;

"Well, call your mom."

I was shocked. "Call my mom? I'm not gonna call my mom!"

At the time, I was running my ad agency. And this is many years ago. It was before social media, I had to go for big clients that could spend lots of money on marketing. I was looking for multi-million dollar to billion dollar companies. I was looking for marketing directors, chief marketing officers, and C-level executives.

That's who I was looking for as leads. So you can imagine my reaction when I'm being told to call my mom, *"Are you freaking kidding me?!!" I'm going to call my mom, and my mom's going to help me get a marketing director? YEAH RIGHT!"*

He responds with, "Well then, just hang up. Why did you call me?"

The guy was on me that day. I said, "No, no, no. I want your help but give me some real advice." Then he said, "I am giving you REAL ADVICE. **Call your mom.**"

I said, "Look, I'm not gonna call my mom." He said, "Well, then I'm not going to give you any other advice, because this is it." I said, "Fine. I'll call my mom."

I continued, "So tell me what we're gonna do." He said, "Are you gonna call your mom?" I said, "Yes, I'll call my mom. I need to say hi to her anyway." He said, "You're gonna call your mom?" I said, "Yes!"

He was making me commit. Or he wouldn't help me with the next step.

"Okay, I'll call my mom but you gotta tell me what to say," I told him. And this is what he proceeded to say.

He said, *"You call your mom and you tell her how excited you are in your business right now; What's going on, what's new, and who you're looking to work with. You tell your mom you're so excited to work with marketing directors you figured out that your best clients are companies that are multi-million dollar companies that have marketing directors that you can talk to."*

So I call my mom (I'll tell you, I was pretty shocked) and on that phone call she gave me two leads of people I should talk to and by the end of the week she had called me back and said, "Steve, I thought of one more."

"Okay, mom, thanks!" But this is the best part. I meet this one guy. This guy worked at the same company with my mom about 20 years previously, and over the years he worked his way up all the way to being a marketing director for another big company in the San Francisco Bay area.

They kept exchanging holiday cards all these years, and so when my mom gave me the man's contact information and I call him, he responded with, *"Oh, I like your mom. I'll meet with you."*

This is before I did 10-minute calls by the way. So I just book an appointment right away and I meet with him. He's like, "You know, I really don't know why we're meeting, but I do like your mom. What's up?"

But by the end of that meeting I had a client. And it was my biggest client for the whole year!

My mom led to my biggest client.

Thanks, Mom.

Just think about the people that you know, and when Trevor was saying who are the contacts you have? Add it all up.

EXERCISE

Write down all the names and contacts of people you know. Don't stop until the table is filled out. Fill out each grid. Look at your Facebook, LinkedIn, Phone Contact etc.

Don't stop. I just want you to feel how much easier it gets as you just *fill out* the cells now. And when you run out of room below, start a spreadsheet.

I have clients who tell me, "I only have 300 people in my phone, so how am I going to reach 1,400+ people in a whole year?"

Then add up your Facebook, your LinkedIn, all the other things that you do, and don't forget it's going to lead to other people. My mom led to three.

If you have 600 people and you multiply that by three, that's 1,800 potential people!

I called one of my friends from high school, and we hadn't talked in years. He went into the military, and we had limited contact through the years.

When I was looking at my phone to find someone to call, I was literally going from A to Z in my contacts. I stopped at James Albertson.

So I call James, "Hey, buddy." We caught up for about 10-minutes. Other than finding out about my business, nothing happened in terms of business transactions. Then later, guess what I found out?

He ended up working his way all the way up to a Vice President (VP) position at a big billion dollar corporation!

We hang up the phone, and he calls me back two days later. He tells me, "I was just at my board meeting and I just realized that the marketing director at my company doesn't know exactly what to do to take the business to the next level, and I think I want to introduce you to him."

Well, guess what? It became a half a million dollar deal for me! A half a million dollar deal from a high school friend that I hadn't talked to for three years!

I just want you to get an idea that you can virtually call anyone because it's not about that person necessarily.

It's about who they know and if they care about you, like my friend from high school did (and my mom)—they're most likely going to work to try to help you.

So you never know! Just get the names on the list. Because in the coming chapters, we are going to show you what to say, so you are respectful, and don't come across as salesy, pushy, or as if you are cold calling.

FOUR - CALL YOUR MOM

> ## Call Your Mom
>
> Create your LIST of people to call.
>
> Tell your mom how excited you are about your business.
>
> Tell her what's going on, what's NEW,
> & WHO you want to work with.

Key Takeaways

- The main DISCIPLINE you need for this process, as Trevor says, is to; **SET appointments and KEEP appointments.**

- **There are many ways to set appointments.** You can make a phone call (like Steve and Robyn do), you can text someone (like Trevor sometimes does), or even use Facebook, Snapchat and other social media platforms (like Steve does.) But the key thing is; pick one, and do it. You can also test different ways, track it and see which method works best.

- You never know how close you are going to be to a HOT LEAD. All you need to realize, is that **anyone can help you.** Whether it be a school friend you haven't spoken to for a long time, or even your mom!

- **Don't make up stories about your leads.** Don't assume they are not of any use to you, don't want your business, or don't want to give you their time. If not, you waste time and energy making up stories that don't serve your business. Just write down their names.

CHAPTER

FIVE

FIVE
What to Say

"The difference between the right word and the almost right word is the difference between lightning and the lightning bug."
—Mark Twain

TREVOR & ROBYN:

"Hey, Joe, it's me. Are you busy? Can you do me a big favor when you have 15 minutes in front of your computer?"

(NOTE: If you choose to invest in our 1 Hour to 6 Figures course, you will really hear Robyn & Trevor singing together.)

STEVE:

They really are singing. Robyn, even gets her guitar out for you. She's pretty good too.

TREVOR:

Yes, we just sang to you the "Make Money" song.

The lyrics we just shared, are all you need to set an appointment with someone, and do that connection call. Yes, we said 15 minutes. But the connection call is shorted. You can change it to 2 minutes.

Just to recap. This is a phone call. And the song lyrics are the script. So I'm going to give you that script now. It's like this:

Your Script

"Hey Joe [Insert person's name], it's me. Are you busy? Can you do me a big favor? When you have 15 [or a couple of] minutes in front of your computer?"

A friend of mine and I used this script to train a group of hundreds, and then thousands of consultants and sales people, who didn't like sales.

They used this script and all they were doing was setting a time to get 15 minutes with someone in front of their computer. You can do the same too, and fill in the blank.

Remember the purpose of this call is to just connect (two minutes) and then set the next appointment (the ten-minute call). That's all you've got to do. You're going to set a timer of one to two minutes.

Set a timer for two minutes. If two minutes go by and haven't set your appointment you hang up, literally. This puts the pressure on to really make this call short. Everyone has things to do, so making this call quick respects everyone.

Also notice, the questions we asked them has just a yes or no answer. "Are you busy?"

You don't want to talk to them about the weather or your dog or about sports or anything else. You're there for one purpose, to set the appointment, and move on to the next person and set another appointment.

Remember, you always have another appointment because in another couple of minutes before your timer runs out, you've got to hang up the phone and call your next person.

Think of this as a checklist. You just want to check them off.

If they answer yes, or they answer no it's okay. Either answer is fine. You're good if they say yes and you're good if they say no.

For example, you might have interrupted them in the middle of their day, so they might respond, "Yes I'm busy."

You then respond, "Okay that's no problem. I just have time for a quick call. Can you do me a favor?"

Then they're going to say, "Sure, what is it?" or "I don't know what you're talking about."

Then you say, "When do you have 10-minutes for quick phone call, where we can just reconnect and find out what each of us is doing. I know we may need more time to fully catch-up, but at least we can connect for 10-minutes."

And that's it. You're setting the appointment. You asked them *when*. You're presupposing that they'll say yes.

"WHEN" Is the key word. You have to PRESUPPOSE they will say YES.

"So when do you have time for a quick call or a cup of coffee, or a time that we can meet and get together?" You can use this in a lot of contexts. We like to do the quick ten-minute call (second stage of the sale) so you don't waste a lot of time talking to the wrong people.

Remember, it's only one hour a day to six figures or more. Doing things as we show you saves time and maximizes return.

Once you set the next call (10-minute call) as part of the connection call, you're going to find out real quickly on the 10-minute call, whether or not that's going to serve you.

I mentioned the possibility of hanging up the phone if your timer goes off and two minutes have gone by. You want to go ahead and literally hang up the phone because that means you lost control of the conversation.

If you lose control of the conversation you can also get confused about what step you're in. That's why I say, you hang up the phone literally, if the two-minute timer goes off.

Most people think I'm joking about this when I share it with them. They think, "Isn't that RUDE Trevor?"

No. You have a schedule to stick to. Even if you hang up the phone, the next time you call, you can say with integrity, *"I'm sorry I cut the last call short. I just want to confirm when we're going to speak on the phone for a quick 10-minute call."* Or you can call back immediately and say, *"I hit the hang up button."* Which happens by accident sometimes. Then get right to setting the appointment. Believe me once you've done this once or twice, you will stick to the time. A lot of people don't have time to catch-up as they'd like to, so truly making this quick helps everyone.

Now I got one last little piece of advise. It's really easy to lead somebody if you use a question that's "like this *or* that".

Give you an example. You might say, *"When's the best time for us to jump on the phone for a quick 10-minute call? Would you like to do it this week or next week?"*

Notice you give them a choice. But either way, it presuppose *they will* jump on a call with you.

You could also use it for more specific times on the calendar. You can say, *"Would you like to do it at 2 o'clock or at 4 o'clock?"*

It's a really nice thing because it gives people a choice in your request. Make it easy for them.

Your Script

*"When is the best time for us to jump on the phone for a quick 10-minute call?
Would you like to do it [Time 1] or [Time 2]?"*

This is a script that you can use. You literally write it on a scrap of paper, keep It in front of you, have your timer there ready, and have your list of people to call in front of you too.

If they respond with, "I don't know" or "No, neither of those will work for me." You simply respond with, "Okay, what's the best time for you?"

You're committed to the call. So you must get them committed to the next step too.

Then go have fun! Because *fun* is what it's all about!

See you in the next chapter.

The Make Money Song

Hey Joe, it's me.

Are you busy?

Can you do me a BIG favor?

When do you have 15 minutes in front of your computer?

Key Takeaways

- The objective of setting appointments, is to get their commitment. Remember the keywords, "when" and "this or that." These all presuppose the person will say yes to your request for a ten-minute call. The word choice is key.

- Whether the lead says yes or no, you're all good. You keep it flowing. You can either speak to them immediately, or later. Remember, with the right script, it presupposes that eventually you will get to talk.

- Always have your script, timer, and list of people to call in front of you. Set a timer for the two-minute call. If two minutes is up, hang up. You don't want to waste time. You want to be in control of your time. You can call the person right back and say, "sorry to disconnect. I've got to run now. When can we connect for 10-minutes?"

CHAPTER

SIX

SIX
Having Fun

"My general attitude to life is to enjoy every minute of every day. I never do anything with a feeling of, 'Oh God, I've got to do this today.'"
—Richard Branson

ROBYN:

Hey, we just wanted to congratulate you. You're halfway there!

STEVE:

Halfway!

TREVOR:

Halfway, alright! (*Trevor is cheering*)

ROBYN:

The fact that you got up to this chapter, means that you are really committed to these results. So many start a book, don't act, and stop before they even reach halfway.

They don't realize the small forward steps that you take make all the difference.

STEVE:

That's right. Sometimes, I tell people: have you seen *Karate Kid* and he's washing the car, he's waxing the car, painting the fence, sanding the deck, and then he gets really mad. He's like "What does this have to do with karate?"

Then all of a sudden, he goes to Mr. Miyagi who shows him that all the movements he's been practicing are blocks?

(*Trevor pretends to attack Steve, and Steve does the "wax on" and "wax off" block*)

STEVE:

See that? I blocked Trevor because I know how to wash the car, did you see that? "I washed Trevor's hand away!" *(Steve, Trevor, and Robyn laugh)*

Now, you might be thinking, "I'm getting all these pieces, but I need to put it all together." We will put it all together for you. By the end, you'll all be ninjas.

ROBYN:

Karate kids.

TREVOR:

Karate kid *and* ninjas!

STEVE:

Okay. So, we're going to give this over to Trevor and he's going to take you to the next step.

TREVOR:

All right, let's do it!

Let's make this fun. Because sometimes when you have to keep the discipline of just picking up the phone, set appointments, and there are other things you would rather be doing. It can get boring and tedious.

The problem is, if you have boring and tedious energy, that comes across to the person you are speaking to. And no one wants to hang out with low energy people.

You must get in a great emotional state, so you can enjoy the process, and the people you call will enjoy having a connection with you, too.

As Dale Carnegie says, *"People rarely succeed unless they are having fun in what they are doing."*

So, I'm going to share a tool that I use to make it all fun. Look at the diagram below.

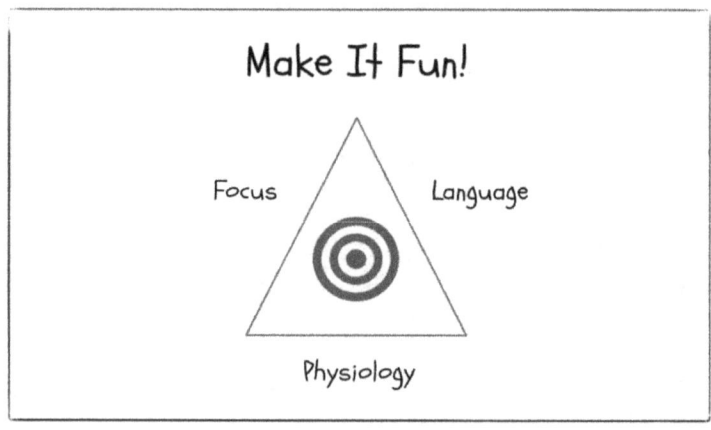

In the very center of this triangle, I like to think of it as a target. Now you can draw on there, whatever you want. You might want to draw in a money sign because you think you want to make some money. That's totally great; you can put that in there.

Sometimes, I'll put a heart on there because it's reminding me that I love and care for the people that I'm reaching out to and I want to help them. Most of the time what I'll do is I'll draw a smiley face because if I'm going to spend this one hour a day and have this discipline, I want to make sure I remember to have fun.

Enjoy the process because you can't control other people, but you can control yourself.

This will give you clarity. Having fun, at the center of the triangle, is about being supported on all three sides.

On the left, we have the gift, the contribution. Because the highest form of contribution you can make to another human being is taking time out of your busy schedule to connect with someone and focus on them. That is a gift. Then help them where you can, if you can.

This means you can't be lazy. It means you have to get up and do it. And if you are, you may as well enjoy it!

Now on the bottom part of this triangle, I remember my physiology. I declare and decide how I want to be.

Here is why it's important: If you were about to make these phone calls and your physiology communicated, "This sucks, I don't want to do it, I've got other things I want to do." And you're all bummed out because you're someone who hates making these calls and doesn't want to do it...

How's that going to affect your calls? How's that going to affect the way that you're impacting and helping other people? Probably not too awesome.

What I like to do is just remember *who do I want to be* if I'm going to show up as my best, to help someone.

For me, it's typically when I'm connected, that I'm congruent, and that I'm confident. I know those are the three C words;

Connected. Congruent. Confident.

I want to be totally confident because I don't want to convince someone. I want to show up very centered. I also want to feel congruent. I don't want to try to push someone else.

You want to make sure that you are attracted to these calls and that you enjoy this and have fun in deciding who you're going to be.

Now, the next thing that I'll focus on is who can you help? This question is about helping you find your perfect target client:

"Who do you know that I can help?"

Remember, it's all about helping people by sharing your gift. It's on the side of the triangle, alongside "gift" and "help."

On the right side of the diagram, I have written "MMS." This just means "Make Money Song," which is the script I gave you in the previous chapter **on What to Say**.

If you use the Make Money Song, you know exactly what you're going to say. Or, if you want to script your message slightly differently, you write it down and have it somewhere you can see. This will help you tremendously.

Over to Steve.

STEVE:

Yeah, I was just going to add one thing real quick. When I'm working with many of my clients before they get going, a lot of them say they don't want to make these calls. Or they don't want to reach out because they don't want to take from somebody else.

I just wanted to be sure that you heard what Trevor said. You're not picking up the phone to say: *"Oh Trevor, give me money. Please."* No, I'm going to be confident and centered that I can HELP people.

Now I'm not 100 percent that I can help Trevor. But that's what I'm going to find out. That's what we're going to talk about. And we'll talk about what language to use for that. But I know in my mind that I'm going to give Trevor a gift.

So, I'm going to focus on how I can help Trevor. This is the focus to give people gifts and help them out.

I believe you have gifts to share. You do. Or you wouldn't be reading this book. So, start giving your gifts away.

What Making Calls Really Means

Making Calls + Giving Gifts = Helping People

TREVOR:

Let me jump in. I want to share the superhero story Robyn shared with me awhile back.

If you ever think of Superman, Superman is not out there on the street assaulting people that are walking down the street.

He's Clark Kent and he's looking around; he stays in disguise until somebody's out there going: "Help!" Then he changes into Superman. But meantime, he's looking out to see how he can be of service.

Your job, when you're making these calls is to make it fun, is to remember that. Your job is to be a superhero.

You want to sort through and find the people who need your help. That's all you're doing. If they don't want your help and/or they don't want to talk to you. Then don't want to receive your gift at this time, or ever. Allow yourself to be cool with that.

Robyn: I want to add something, too. If they don't need your help, find out who does. They know someone who needs your help. Ask someone, "Know anyone who is calling for help?"

Trevor: That's a good point. Glad you brought it up, Robyn. Even if someone doesn't need your help, they might know someone who does.

If you're on a call with someone, you can ask them "Who do you know we can help?" <u>We</u> is an important word in that question, because when they refer you they are helping too.

Remember, have fun! You're a superhero! And there are people waiting to receive your gift. You just have to find them.

SIX - HAVING FUN

> # 7 Magic Words Words
>
> Who
> Do
> You
> Know
> We
> Can
> Help?

Key Takeaways

- Make sure you are in the right state (like California… no just kidding. The Right State of Mind…) to make the calls. You want to have fun. You want to bring positive energy to your interaction with whomever you are speaking to. Make the calls an activity you look FORWARD to!

- Calling people doesn't mean you are bothering them. It just means you care enough that you want to connect, to see how you can help, and to share your gift(s). It's about being of service.

- Your job in making calls, is to be a superhero. You don't force what you have on other people. You are discovering if they have a need and they want help. And even if they don't, someone they know probably does. And with the right connection and confidence, you can ask them for a referral.

CHAPTER

SEVEN

SEVEN
10-Minute Calls

*"Sales are contingent upon the attitude of the salesman
—not the attitude of the prospect."*
—W. Clement Stone

STEVE:

All right, we've been talking about this <u>10-Minute Call</u> throughout this book.

What is it?

When I get on the phone after a two-minute call (let's say it's with Trevor), and schedule a 10-minute call, the first thing I want to do is say:

"Hey, remember we set 10-minutes for this call. What I was thinking is I can share what I'm up to, and I wanted to get to know what you're up to. Sound good?"

TREVOR:

That's cool.

STEVE:

This is important. You set the time expectation up front (10-minutes), and you also make clear what you want to get out of the call, and what you want from them. Simple.

STEVE:

Then the next thing I'm going to do, is I'm going to use what I call an **Audio Logo**. This is something I teach in my book *Capture Clients Close Deals*, and Trevor teaches, too.

What's the Audio Logo? It's a 30-60 second summary of: who you are, who you work with and their typical challenges, and what results you help them get.

Done right, you can communicate those three parts in less than a minute. You literally "let them know what you're up to" in seconds. Here's a sample:

"Hi, I'm Steve. Typically, I work with entrepreneurs, C-level executives, and coaches/consultants, who have reached success, yet they are challenged with not having the lifestyle they want... They have yet to solve this and they feel alone in finding a way to break away from work. I've helped my clients design their life first and then systematize their business around that, to reach millions of dollars in new revenue. I help them gain more business and more life."

TREVOR:

This is huge, guys. Steve just gave a great Audio Logo that was very specific in who he typically works with, the challenges that they have, and then the results that he brings them. So, that's the **Audio Logo**.

STEVE:

And now if Trevor was my prospect, he is going to be like, *"Wow. That's frickin pretty cool!"*

I'm not even 60 seconds into the call. I have more than nine minutes left! And the rest of the nine minutes, I'm going to spend focusing on Trevor, or whoever I am talking to. Because I really want to know what's going on for *them*, to see if I can help.

And if there's nothing I can help him (Trevor) with, maybe I can refer him to somebody else. Maybe I can tell him, *"Hey you know what? I would Google this."*

I'm just giving them some tips even if there's no reason for us to work together. Remember, it's all about being of service, whether the person works with you or not.

I might then say to them, *"Do you know anyone who might be a good fit? Do you know any entrepreneurs that have some success, but don't have the life they want?"* I'm able to ask that question. And because I'm being helpful, they will, most likely want to be helpful to me, too.

TREVOR:

Let's recap. You clear some time in your calendar. You set an intention and purpose for the call (service, fun etc.), and you are going to create and use your Audio Logo.

Create Your Audio Logo

"Typically I work with [insert who you work with] who are [insert their main pains, struggles, challenges]. After working with me, my clients/customers have gained [insert results]."

STEVE:

I also want to add one more thing. I love saying the 10-minute call up front, because then Trevor (or the prospect) knows, "Well, I can do 10-minutes. It's only 10-minutes, and Steve is a good friend/nice guy, etc."

Then Trevor or the prospect will say, "Sure." Then I share my Audio Logo.

Who do I work with? Entrepreneurs, C-level executives, and coaches/consultants

What's going on for them? They have reached success, yet they are challenged with not having the lifestyle they want... They **have yet to solve this** and they feel **alone in finding a way to break away from work**.

What do I do for them? I've helped my clients design their life first and then systematize their business around that, to reach millions of dollars in new revenue. I help them gain more business and more life

And then I might even say, "And you know what? My biggest goal is to gain more speaking engagements right now so that I can help more people. The more people I get in front of, the more people I can serve."

Then the other person, for example, Trevor, knows *exactly* what I'm up to, and what I'm looking for.

Now the rest of the conversation is about the other person. At this stage, I'm probably at most two minutes into the conversation. I have at least eight minutes to learn about the prospect. In this example, that prospect is Trevor.

TREVOR:

Nice. Also, I want to add something here. We are also going to teach you and ask you to use something called **Keyword Backtracking**.

STEVE:

The **Keyword Backtracking** is important because Trevor might say things differently than me. Remember I said, "A lot of entrepreneurs are alone." But he might say, "I feel like I'm by myself these days."

If he's talking about a pain that he has, I'm not going to say, "Alone", because that's *my* word. I'm going to say, "Oh you feel like you're **by yourself.**" I'm going to use *his* words.

When I use Trevor's words, he is going to feel like I really am listening to him, and that I really do understand. Listening and understanding is a must, so you really are going to want to do that. The keyword backtracking lets them know you are listening. Almost all the time, they don't notice consciously that you are backtracking the keywords. Sub-consciously they notice. Note: Don't repeat everything they say, just the keywords or points. All the words would be strange and could come off as mockery. You are not trying to copy or mimic them. You are honoring they're language and you are just making sure you got the keywords right. This will build a lot of rapport.

Use their keywords NOT yours.

TREVOR:

That's right. Just because two words might mean the same thing to you, it does not mean it means the same thing to someone else. If they say, "great," and you say, "awesome," that is not the same thing.

If they say that they're "struggling" right now and you were to just take the gist of that and say, "Oh, it must be really hard for you." Then they may feel like you don't understand them fully.

STEVE:

And you should have the script in front of you so let's just do it, and you follow along as we do it.

Let's go back to talking to Trevor as if he's my prospect. *"It makes me really curious because goals are so important to me. I'm curious; what's your biggest goal this year, Trevor?"*

TREVOR:

"My biggest goal this year is to get a hundred people a month buying into my new Best Seller Big Business online course and program. I've got a webinar that drives people to it, and I just want to get to where I'm doing a hundred people a month consistently. That's the biggest goal I've got this year."

STEVE:

Okay, so you want to get a hundred people coming to your course per month?

TREVOR:

"Mm hmm. Correct. People signing up and buying the course every single month."

STEVE:

Then I'll respond with, *"Awesome. It makes me more curious, so <u>when</u> you have that, what <u>will</u> having that do for you?"*

TREVOR:

(Continuing the role play…) "That's a great question, Steve. Every day, I write this down and it's going to help give me everything I want as far as the financial freedom and then also the time freedom that I want with my family. And it's also creating a new process that I can give to all of my clients."

STEVE:

"Wow, that's awesome, Trevor!"

Okay, let's pause and break it down a little here. So, by me asking the magical question, "What will having that do for you?" Trevor gave me lots of rich information.

He'll have more in his life.

He'll be able to help more people. He's going to be able to teach his clients even more. There was more heart in that than anything, so now he's feeling like, "Wow, this is awesome."

I want you to use the exact words, too. **"What will having that do for you?"**

TREVOR:

And, you're always going to want to probe a little deeper. So, let's give you another example. Say someone tells you, *"I want to lose 20 pounds."*

STEVE:

Then I would say, "When you lose 20 pounds, what will having that do for you?"

TREVOR:

The other person might say, *"Well, when I lose 20 pounds, I will look better when I go to my high school reunion and I'll feel proud of myself instead of embarrassed about my body."*

STEVE:

Notice how much deeper that is. The person's main emotional desire is to feel proud, instead of embarrassed. That gives you very important information, which deals with much more than simply losing 20 pounds.

I also want to add, you might be able to ask this question more than once. You might ask it again, "So, when you go to your high school reunion feeling proud and looking better, what will having that do for you?"

(Note: I backtracked the keywords, "Feeling proud and looking better when you go to your high school reunion.")

TREVOR:

And they might respond with, "I can finally feel respected in my life." How sweet is that?

This continued curiosity, digging a little deeper, allowing you to find the emotion. And you want to figure out the emotion of what they want, or what they don't want.

STEVE:

Absolutely. So, let's move on. Back to the role play with Trevor. *"Trevor, what thing do you think is most slowing you down or stopping you from hitting that hundred a month?"*

TREVOR:

"The one thing we're focused on right now is finding the right audience online. We're targeting Facebook and LinkedIn, and just driving the right marketing and advertising to them. We had someone on our team doing it for us.

We need someone new to do it for us. We just need to clean it up. There's not much, but right now it's finding the right person and the right audience and the right message, I guess."

STEVE:

"So, you are focused on finding the right audience online and that's slowing you down?"

TREVOR:

"Yeah."

STEVE:

"And with having that happen, how does that affect you right now?"

(This question helps me understand what his main emotional experience is *now*.)

TREVOR:

"Well, not having it in place makes me feel like I haven't done my homework. I feel bad. Like there's something I've done wrong because I know there are a lot of people who need our program. And because I'm in the process of figuring it out, I'm frustrated.

I wanted it to happen last month and so that makes me feel that I've been lazy, when I've not been lazy. It's just frustrating."

STEVE:

As Trevor says that, his state changes, too. His voice softens; he looks down, and the curve on his mouth is more downward than upward. With this information, I *know* he is getting into the emotion of not having what he wants yet.

The reason we're hitting on these emotions is because then people will be present to what they are feeling, and to be present with it. This gets them reaching for a solution.

TREVOR:

Agreed. So, even if Steve and I were to end the call right now, it definitely got me thinking.

STEVE:

Absolutely. Because now he's thinking about where he wants to go. We just elicited the positive emotion and now the negative emotion.

The polarity causes movement. Just like electricity flows when you have a positive and a negative terminal. You have to have this polarity.

Now I can say to Trevor, *"Trevor, because I know you want these hundred clients a month, and you want that to come every month. Right now, finding the right audience on Facebook and LinkedIn is causing issues. And that's exactly what I've helped my clients with before.*

Remember I told you I've helped them reach millions more in revenue? I've done exactly that. I'm not sure if I can help you. I might be able to. With all the things I've done, it feels pretty right. I'm curious, is that something you may want help with?"

TREVOR:

"Yeah."

STEVE:

What I've done is I am inviting him to take the next step, which is the *discovery call*. So, what I'd say now is:

"What I want to discover is if that's true. If I can help you. Because I don't want to take up too much of either of our time, if I can't help you.

But I would want to make a solid recommendation. Because even if it's not me, I have some friends that maybe I could refer you to."

"What we should do is set up a Discovery Call, where we'd have more than 10-minutes, and I can dig a little bit deeper about what's going on and see precisely if I can help you or not.

Would you want to do that?"

TREVOR:

"Yeah."

STEVE:

"Okay, so what day is good for you? I could do Tuesday at 10am or Wednesday at 3:30pm."

(Notice that I used what Trevor showed you in a different chapter, which is the "this or that" language.)

TREVOR:

Ha ha! *(Trevor is laughing…)*

STEVE:

Then Trevor will pick one time.

But what if Trevor wanted something else, like socks to keep his feet warm, then I wouldn't be the guy to help him out on a discovery call.

Though I can tell him that I heard XYZ company makes good socks. Or, maybe he could go to Amazon and buy them and have it shipped to him overnight. I can make a recommendation to Trevor, so I'm always helpful.

Whether Trevor brings anything to me or not, at least I'm giving him a gift. Because the whole point is giving gifts.

Then in return, I can make a request. I can ask Trevor, "Hey, who in your world do you know that has speaking opportunities to get in front of entrepreneurs or C-level executives?

TREVOR:

So, next up in the book, we are going to talk about the *discovery call*.

And if you have any questions in the meantime, just reach out to either myself, Steve or Robyn. We have plenty of resources and courses to help you take the next step!

Audio Logo

Typically, I work with _____

Who have the challenge of _____

And I help them get _____

Key Takeaways

- The audio logo is a simple 30-60 second script, that communicates; who you work with, their typical challenges, and the typical results you help people get.

- The purpose of a 10-minute call, is to see if you are a match, then you can move them to a discovery call.

- Whether they go for the discovery call or not, make sure you are helpful. Give them a gift. Because it's all about being of service.

- Keyword backtracking is about using their words to build rapport with them.

- Use the scripts to get the emotional experience of both what they want and what they don't want. Get both positive and negative emotion.

- Even if someone doesn't book a discovery call, with enough trust and rapport, you can ask them to refer you to someone who they know might want your service or product. Or someone they know might be able to help out with what you want. It's win-win.

CHAPTER

EIGHT

EIGHT
Discovery Calls

*"Approach each customer with the idea of helping him
or her solve a problem or achieve a goal,
not of selling a product or service."*
—Brian Tracy

ROBYN:

Welcome to Chapter 8. This is all about the Discovery Call. What you just learned was specifically what you could do during the 10-minute call.

It's going to be a quick call to really find out if they're a possible good prospect for you. If so, then you want to find out what is the next step for them.

How are you going to work with them? You need to go through this process. Again, as we mentioned, you can always skip steps, but you want to know what step is next so you know what to drive them to. Most the time, you are not going to skip steps. I only do this, when I know the person really wants to work with me and I feel it is a good fit. Then I may be able to take them right to the strategy session. Most the time I follow each step through.

So, it really depends on where they are, how ready they are to take action, and how clearly they have communicated that with you. Most the time if I do skip a step, it is because they come to me asking to be a client.

Okay. The Discovery Call is usually anywhere from 15 to 30 minutes.

I always tell my clients that after 30 minutes, because this is usually a free call, after 30 minutes every minute after that your credibility actually goes down.

You're giving this free time, you've already spent 10-minutes with them and so you want to make sure to keep your credibility up. It's got to stay short. If for any reason, you do go over 30 minutes, you want to give them a reason.

"Wow, because I think you're really great, we might work together, and it seems like this could be a good fit...and so I want to spend extra time with you. Is that okay?"

You just want to make sure this doesn't get super long because you want to drive them to the next step, which is actually the paid strategy session that Trevor is going to go over in the next chapter.

It's where you get money for your time and still make sure to figure out whether or not they're a client for something further. Cool huh?

Here's what you need to do during a discovery session, however. I broke it down, the sales process, into 4 steps so it's super easy. I call it the FCC.

FCC stands for Frustrations, Concerns, and Challenges

"What are your frustrations, concerns, and challenges when it comes to [insert answer]?"

The discovery call is all about digging into the pain.

You started that process a little bit earlier in the 10-minute call when you asked them, *"What's stopping you or holding you back from getting what you want?"*

Now's your chance to dig a little bit deeper.

Of course, you only have 20-30 minutes so you're not going to go crazy deep into it. But you want to make sure there's something they don't want to continue and that gives you leverage to get them to take action.

The question you ask is as follows:

What are the primary frustrations, concerns and challenges you're facing right now?

Or if you want to be elaborate a bit, you can ask:

So, on our last call you told me that you wanted [Insert WANT] and that you were experiencing [Insert PAIN.] What are your frustrations, concerns, and challenges when it comes to [insert WANT]?

The answer all depends on what information you got in the previous 10-minute call. It could be weight loss. It could be about gaining more clients. Whatever it is, you insert that in the script.

Then ZIP it and listen. You can take notes but, you also want to capture their keywords so you can backtrack it to them later. Just like how Steve and Trevor taught you in the last chapter. You can keyword backtrack the key pains and ask "How does that affect you?" That will take it even deeper.

Got it? Awesome. Let's move on.

Once you've done FCC you want to transition into MW.

Once you know the pain, you want to find out what is it they really want? The script is as follows.

MW stands for Magic Wand

"If you could wave a magic wand, what would you like with regards to your [insert what they are working on, be it: business, health, relationships, etc.]?"

Then you let them just tell you their answer. They will paint the picture for themselves as to what they really, really want.

There are a couple of things that happen when you ask the magic wand question. There's a part of your brain called the "Critter Brain" or the "Lizard Brain." Its job is to keep you safe. Its job is to have you survive, not to thrive. This part of the brain does not care about quality of life; all it cares about is the quantity of life. By allowing it to say, "This is just magic, it's not real," it allows them to explore.

A lot of people always think of what's possible because it seems survivable. What this "magic wand" question does, is it tricks the critter brain to say, "Hey. No. Anything is possible. Just tell me. What do you want? Dream. If you could wave a magic wand, what would you have?"

Then the critter brain doesn't just try to protect you the whole time and leave you in fear.

Second, by asking them the question, you get them to dream; you have them dream big, and you also get them to attach some positive emotions to it. They get a hint of the pleasure of having what they want, if they could wave a magic wand.

You can then keyword backtrack what they are dreaming they want and ask "What will having that do for you?" Once again, this dips you into the emotions behind the want.

Next, we go to the YES LADDER.

The Yes Ladder is the transition to the offer. All you do here is ask at least three "yes" questions.

The Yes Ladder

1. Has this been valuable so far?
2. Does this make sense?
3. Do you see how this will help you [**backtrack the keywords to the benefit they want**]?

Typically, they're going to say yes. If not, you can always go back and find out what's going on, but you want to get a yes.

Again, the job of the Yes Ladder is to tell that fear part of your brain, the part that's just trying to keep you safe, to distract that part of your brain and tell the critter brain, "Do not get in my way."

Your job is to help the person get what they want, not to let them sit in the same fear that they've been in for years—if not decades—of their life. Which is why they're not where they want to be.

Now, the last part is the OFFER to take the next step. We teach this in all our courses. Trevor, Steve, and I. We have many courses that help people learn to make irresistible offers.

I have that in my FEMM Mentorship™ program. I know Trevor has that in his Best Seller Big Business program. Steve has that in his More Business More Life program. There are all sorts of ways you can get very, very clear on your packaging and your offer, and how to make it irresistible.

The main thing about the offer is that you want to anchor the value high and really show that there's great value if they work with you.

Then you want to give them a discounted rate. You're not doing this to be a jerk. You're not making up some crazy high value.

People love to buy and get a discount. They love to buy "on sale." They want a great deal. You want to give them that opportunity.

The next step is the Strategy Session. This is the next stage of the sale. It is a paid session. Trevor will speak more about this in the next Chapter.

TREVOR:

I want to add something before we finish this chapter. Yes, you want to make your strategy session offer irresistible, and a discount is one of the ways to do it. But you can also add bonuses instead of discounting. These are bonuses they only get if they sign up for your strategy session.

It's all about creating more VALUE. Whether you discount, or you add bonuses. It's about making it compelling. It's about making it irresistible.

ROBYN:

That's great. Thanks Trevor. I'm glad you added that.

STEVE:

One other thing to note here, is to offer a risk reversal. This is where you take the risk, by giving them a money back guarantee. There is a fee for the strategy session or whatever you call this session, so you can say, "If you don't feel you got value from the Strategy Session, just let me know during or at the end of the session and I'll give you your money back." They have to tell you on that call.

That is my policy. You don't want them to come back to you weeks or months later. If they ask on the spot I will give them a refund. By the way, I've only had one refund from a strategy session out of hundreds. If you follow the steps Trevor is going to give you, they will gain value and be thankful they paid you for it.

ROBYN:

As Steve mentioned, what we call the "Strategy Session" doesn't have to be called a strategy session.

Trevor will go over what that means. It can be an intermediary step. One of my clients that I mentioned earlier are architects and their thing was to offer a design consult where they got paid some money for it. So, they call it a design consult.

But the important thing is, you have to understand that it is a stage of the sale. And that the strategy session stage, is a paid session. You get them to pay you a little bit of money.

TREVOR:

Agreed.

You could even call it a Soul Session. I know Steve was saying one of his clients is very connected and spiritual, and they call it a Soul Session. I have a Book Building Session or a Book Strategy Session. But these are all *paid* sessions.

ROBYN:

Correct. You are training them to understand that when they pay you, they get value. And you're going to deliver more value than what they pay for.

It's the stepping stone they need to get to the high-ticket item, which is to engage you and become your paying client.

Discovery Calls

___ CLEAR THE TIME
___ SET THE INTENTION
___ BUILD RAPPORT

1. FCC
   What are your primary Frustrations, Concerns and Challenges?

2. Magic Wand
   If you could wave a magic wand, what would you like?
   (Or how would it be?)

3. YES LADDER (Ask at least 3 "yes" questions)
   Has this been valuable so far?
   Does this make sense?
   Do you see how much this will help you grow your business?
   Do you see how this will help you _____, _____, _____?

4. Offer
(You want to anchor the "value" high so they feel like their getting a great deal. You can offer a discount, &/or offer bonuses, but your goal is to make it irresistible.)

Key Takeaways

- FCC stands for Frustrations, Concerns, and Challenges. You want to understand their pain. People don't take action unless there is urgency. And when there is pain, there is urgency.

- MW stands for Magic Wand. You want them to dream. You want them to feel what it is like to have what they want, without their critter brain firing off their fears. This helps them focus on the outcome of what they want, rather than what they don't have.

- The Yes Ladder is another way to calm their critter, but it also trains your prospect to be in agreement with what you have to offer. Doing this right helps them get closer to their goal. A goal they probably haven't been getting to since no one has worked with them, to calm their critter, and see what is possible.

CHAPTER

NINE

NINE
Strategy Sessions

"Either you run the day or the day runs you."
—Jim Rohn

TREVOR:

Welcome to Chapter 9!

You've been streamlined up until this point. You've gotten clear about your list. You've had fun. You've gone ahead and set appointments and had the discipline to follow through. Now you have someone who really wants to work with you.

In fact, they paid you for the privilege. It's now up to you to give them permission.

We're now going to talk about the Strategy Session. This makes all the magic happen.

A lot of time in the "sales part," people are freaking out, and they're thinking they have to go ahead and pitch. That is the opposite of what we're doing here.

This is not about all the stuff you've got to say. This is about asking the right questions.

You'll notice that pattern. From the very first connection call, to the 10-minute call, to the discovery call—everything is part of a step-by-step system of asking questions to discover your match.

We go into much more detail in this in a variety of different ways.

ROBYN:

Yeah. I just want to add something in regards to the importance of the strategy session. Everything leading up to this, the 10-minute call, the discovery call, the strategy session, if you notice there are some themes in all of those.

Some people ask, *"Well what's the difference between the discovery call, the strategy session, and the 10-minute call?"*

The thing is they're all very similar because of what you're getting to. You're digging to really find out about their problems. Why do you want to know that? Not just to close them. Not just to help them. You want to know that because now you *know how* to help them.

If you don't know the problems that you're solving, first of all, you don't know how to communicate to your potential clients. You also don't know how to solve that problem.

As a financial planner, I really was trying to solve people's problems by giving them a box. For example, the box is a service or a life insurance product.

It didn't work well. Because I didn't really understand the problem. When I really started asking these questions using the 10-minute call, the discovery call, the strategy session—I really understood what they wanted.

I was then able to develop a solution in the form of a system.

Steve talks a lot about this in his book *Capture Clients Close* Deals. This is a simple way to gain clients without convincing or chasing. He calls it *survey to success*.

Any time I have a potential client, I'm really surveying them because I actually get to know what their problems are.

TREVOR:

Thank you, Robyn! Thank you, honey.

So, in this strategy session that you have already been paid for, you are now figuring out how to give people PERMISSION to buy from you.

That's right. You aren't selling. You already have their solution. You are interviewing them to see if they are a right fit.

Now, I want to make something clear. This book isn't about teaching you *how* to sell. It is about the system to use for one hour a day to gain six figures or more.

It's to teach you how to spend their time, how not to use your time, and what questions to ask so you create the opportunity to sell. And that opportunity to sell happens in the strategy session.

This book is about the discipline of the micro-steps that setup that GOLDEN conversation.

If you want to master the strategy session and sales, if you want to know how to sell like a master, you can go ahead and get one of our books or you can attend one of our programs.

My course is called the **Holy Grail of Sales**. Steve's course is called **Discovering A Match**. That's a four-day event. Robyn's course is called **Advanced Sales Mastery**.

We show you how to package and position a service that's PERFECT for your client.

We aren't going to go into too much detail here. But the point is, we want you to understand that you ARE NOT selling a box as Robyn says.

Robyn is now going to the *benchmark* questions you need to ask in the Strategy Session, before leading them to a close. This question is the KEY question you need answered.

Decision Maker

ROBYN:

I call it the "Decision Maker."

The question is: *"Assuming we're to work together in some capacity. Are you the decision maker?"*

Steve calls it something else; we call it this. It doesn't really matter. You want to get a YES to that question. You don't want to go through the whole strategy session, position your offering, and have the prospect say, "Oh, let me check with my husband."

That's called a waste of time for both you and the prospect.

You just need a simple YES or a simple NO. The sooner you find out, the better.

TREVOR:

That also applies to getting a decision from them at the end of the strategy session. Once you position your offering, you want them to be able to clearly decide YES or NO.

You don't want "MAYBE's."

You must have them make a decision. If they are not ready to buy now, if you can't have them as a client, move on. You can make them another recommendation, but then that is it. Move on.

Remember, you have a process. You just follow it. Collect a decision, and move on with the stages of the sale: 2-minute call, 10-minute call, discovery call, strategy session and close.

Regardless of the decision they make, it comes down to two things to remember; *setting appointments*, and *keeping appointments*.

Even if they don't buy. You want to BAMFAM.

BAM FAM: Book A Meeting, From A Meeting.

If at the end of your conversation they're not ready to buy, that's okay. If you still want them to be your client, you need to set that next appointment.

As a rule of thumb, this is a language we use internally with our clients all the time. You want to BAMFAM them after every single point of contact.

If it's not the time right now, you set the next strategy session, or appointment, or time that you're going to follow up. This is really key.

I will share with you what I went through during the first stages of this sales process where I reached out and did the connection call. I went and did the 10-minute call. I did the discovery call. I had this woman, her name is Jen. She said, *"Yes, Trevor. I want your help."*

Then for some reason on the discovery call she pulled back. I wasn't even able to schedule the strategy session.

She sometimes would schedule it and not make it. Now, this is a woman that I have a lot of respect for. I really like. She's one of my perfect clients.

That was okay with me. My job is to just go from one step to the other.

I still wanted her as a client. What I did in that moment when she didn't show up, is I scheduled my next appointment with her. On my own, I decided when I was going to follow up with her. I put her in my calendar and decided I'm going to call her in a month.

Not everybody wants to buy your stuff right now or even has the time to have a call with you.

The really cool thing about this is that she became a client eventually. She now pays me a healthy sum of money because she truly did want my help. It just wasn't the right time.

(Just so you know, this client is worth over $30,000 to me.)

This is someone I definitely wanted to followup with. So I had to have the discipline of booking a meeting from a meeting, until it paid off.

It wasn't hard. But I had to be consistent.

Strategy Sessions

Everything you've done has led you to this session.

This is where you deliver the magic.
The most important thing about this is...

You use a SYSTEM to guide the conversation.

Key Takeaways

- You must find out if they are the decision maker at the start of the strategy session. This is key. Or else you waste time.

- Don't sell a box. People want a solution to their problems, and they want to know that you have that specific solution for them.

- Sales is about asking questions. All stages of the sale are an opportunity to connect, find out more about your prospect, and lead them to make a decision; yes or no.

- Sales is a process. Regardless of whether someone signs up and works with you or not, stick to the stages of the sale. Stick to the system. And keep Booking a Meeting From a Meeting (BAMFAM), as Trevor says.

CHAPTER

TEN

TEN
Do Or Die

"The difference between a successful person and others is not a lack of strength, not a lack of knowledge, but rather a lack of will."
—Vince Lombardi

TREVOR:

Congratulations!

ROBYN:

Yay.

TREVOR:

We're going to talk about a couple of things here really quickly.

Steve, when you mentioned this right at the beginning, it's about making sure that you are committed to playing full out.

STEVE:

Yep. Play full out to get what you want!

TREVOR:

The first thing that you want to do is focus on commitment.

You need to be disciplined. Just an hour a day. You can choose to do that all on Monday if you want. But you must stick to it.

STEVE:

Yeah, one day. I have one client who does all his calls in one day. Then the rest of the week, he works with clients and enjoys his life.

TREVOR:

That's a great idea! You can just block out a whole day and make it happen.

Now, I want to give you the last piece to make it more compelling for you to commit. It's called consequence.

People often need a consequence of not taking action, to make sure that they take action. I've seen it. This works tremendously well for me. I know it's going to work tremendously well for Steve and Robyn, too. And it's worked for our clients.

You've got to make sure you have a self-imposed consequence; something that is going to cost you.

Robyn's got a kind of a fun way of saying it. Robyn, what is it?

ROBYN:

Well, this is how you do goes:

You think of something you don't want to do. That you're willing to do, if you *don't* do what you say you're going to do…

Then you have to do it.

TREVOR:

Here's an example, I wrote my dad a check one time. I decided well, what do I not want to do? I didn't want to send my dad money.

So, I wrote a check and I gave it to my wife. I said, *"Honey, if I don't make my calls this week, send that check to my father."*

Guess what? **I made the calls.**

STEVE:

It doesn't have to be money either.

It could be something else like something you usually do with your family. You can tell them, *"Hey listen, if I don't do these calls, I'm not going to be able to do that with you this weekend."*

Then you must explain yourself to your family. For me that would be huge, because if you know me well, time with my family and kids is precious to me. It drives me to get stuff done so I can be present with them.

If I had to go to my kids and say *"Sorry, daddy can't play with you because I didn't do my homework,"* then I would be devastated.

I can't stand the picture of my kids' eyes looking at me saying, "Why not daddy?"

The whole purpose of the consequence is so that there is something worse if you don't do what you need to do. It's bad that you may not do what you need to, but sometimes it's not bad enough. If it was, you would already be doing it. If there is a consequence that is bad enough, it can motivate you to do it.

TREVOR:

At one time, I set a consequence to run 10 miles. The longest I run when I go jogging or something is two, three, four, or five miles. Those are big runs for me.

I set this 10-mile consequence I was willing to do. And I will admit that there was a time I had to go run 10 miles in a day. It was tough, because I had to be willing to do it and I had to pay the price.

STEVE:

So, the question is, *"What in your world would make you so uncomfortable that it would push you over the edge to get this done?"* To commit to one hour a day?

ROBYN:

I just wanted to add one more thing to clarify.

Here's the thing, you're getting consequences in your life anyway.

If you're in debt or you don't have the money you want, there are consequences.

What we're saying is we have to do a self-imposed consequence.

TREVOR:

It lights a fire under your butt, so it gets you into action!

After you identify the consequences, make a public declaration. Like posting on Facebook. Or declaring it to an accountability partner; significant other, business partner, or friend.

You can say, *"Listen, if I don't do 'this', you have to make sure that I do THIS (consequence)."*

STEVE:

Now, if by chance, consequences don't work and your "will" fades, (willpower only lasts so long), then reach out to me. There are ways to reprogram your mindset around what you want or don't want. Working deeper on your mindset is much better than beating yourself up over and over. Believe me, I know. My first 12 years in business, I did just that and through shifting my mindset and beliefs, I've been able to simply move past what blocked me from doing and having what I want.

ROBYN:

Also, this is not just about negative consequences. You can get creative with this, too, and celebrate positive consequences of your commitment.

I have a FEMM Mentorship, Female Empowered Money Makers mentorship for women and women entrepreneurs. Two of the ladies are twin sisters, architects, and they don't like to spend money. They don't really like to reward themselves.

It was hard to reward themselves, because they're kind of go, go, go in their business. They go take action. They did the consequence, but they didn't want to spend more money, because that felt actually like a consequence.

What they had to do to *force themselves to celebrate was if* they closed X amount of discovery calls and closed X amount of strategy sessions and got X amounts of clients, they set up a whole system, then they could give themselves a certain gift; a massage or a fun day.

It didn't always have to mean spending money, but they'd actually give themselves those gifts for taking action.

STEVE:

We do want to celebrate. One of the first projects Trevor and I worked on together was a restaurant consulting practice.

TREVOR:

We started a restaurant consulting practice. We had a TV show around it called *Project Restaurant*. Steve, Marco (our common friend), and I held a strategy session for a restaurant for one day.

STEVE:

It was to go over the whole strategy of the restaurant itself.

TREVOR:

In this one-day consultation, we went ahead and not only were we paid for that consultation, we made a sale where we partnered with that restaurant to help them with their marketing and to grow their business. It was the three of us.

It was worth over $300,000 of value for us. In one day, we made $300,000 and boy did we celebrate!

STEVE:

Now, because my brother was nearby to this restaurant, we all ended up going to my brother's house.

We were celebrating the whole day. We laughed so hard during the sale, we actually didn't even realize how much money we'd made until we left.

We got in the car and then we're like *"Oh my gosh, this was a $300,000 day."* We each made $100,000 in one day.

I said, "We have to celebrate." So, I called my brother and said, "Hey, get the champagne. We're almost to your house."

We just had a blast. Celebrating lifts your spirits. We looked forward to doing more of what we did!

ROBYN:

That's so awesome!

STEVE:

That's why we celebrate. Because it rewards you to go to the next day, so that you can then do more.

Every time you help one client, you're going to want to go help more clients. Enjoy it, embrace it and do whatever it is.

ROBYN:

This is your chance. Celebrate along the way and we're so happy you took this journey with us in this book.

We also have so much stuff to offer. Aside from our paid program **One Hour a Day to Six Figures**, where you get some live coaching with us, and plenty of other bonuses—we give away a ton of free stuff on our personal websites, too.

For me, you can go to RobynCrane.com.

STEVE:

My website is SteveNapolitan.com.

TREVOR:

You're going to notice a pattern here. Mine is TrevorCrane.com.

STEVE:

We look forward to helping you.

ROBYN:

Thank you and look forward to connecting soon!

STEVE:

And remember, have fun!

Consequence

Q1: What's the "real" consequence you'll suffer if you don't follow through?

Q2: What's your "self imposed" consequence?

Q3: Who is going to hold you accountable?

Reward

Q1: How will you reward yourself when you hit your goals? (Brainstorm ideas. Think of things you love to do.)

Q2: What has to happen in order to get your reward?

Q3: How will you celebrate? Who will you celebrate with?

Key Takeaways

- Both positive and negative reinforcement can be used to support you.

- Setting up consequences to make you take action is a great way to support you in committing to one hour a day of calls.

- Setting up a positive reward, and positive consequences, is also a great way to help you commit to one hour a day of calls.

HERE'S WHAT TO DO NEXT

As we said in the preface of this book, we're going to ask you to do three things:

1. Keep it simple.
2. Commit to one hour a day.
3. Get help.

We are here to help you.

This is not the end; it is only the beginning. You cannot, and should not try to do this all by yourself. The three of us would not be where we are if we didn't get help. We welcome you to reach out to each of us to find out the best way we can help you design the life and the business you ultimately desire.

Enjoy your 1-hour a day. What amazing results that 1-hour creates.

We leave you for now, with much love and gratitude.

—Steve, Robyn and Trevor

ACKNOWLEDGMENTS

There are so many people in our lives who have made a book like this possible. First of all, we'd like to acknowledge the Best Seller Big Business publishing team for all of your diligent hard work, and attention to detail. You are amazing.

We'd also like to thank our families who are our most important people to us on the planet. We don't know what we'd do without you.

Specifically, we'd like to thank, Jon Low, Ashley Peterson and Mariska Rowell.

We'd also like to thank you, the reader.

You are incredible, and more powerful than you can ever imagine. Thank you for trusting us enough to let us be a little part of your journey. If there is ever anything we can do to help you, please let us know. You can find our websites in our bio.

PRODUCTS & PROGRAMS

Achieving "MASTERY" of anything, especially a sales system does not happen over night.

Continue to invest in yourself to get the skills and tools you need to have Sales Mastery.

This way you can you can make more money and help more people.

GET THE COURSE!

1Hour6Figures.com

MASTER SALES

MoreBusinessMoreLife.com

MASTER SALES

ASMEvent.com

MASTER SALES

trevorcrane.com/holygrail

ABOUT THE AUTHORS

Steve Napolitan is an international speaker, best-selling author (Capture Clients Close Deals), trainer, and coach. He has decades of experience in advertising, marketing, and promotions, and has worked with high-profile companies such as Apple, Intel, Charles Schwab, and Nestle.

Typically, Steve works with entrepreneurs, C-level executives, and coaches/consultants who have reached success, yet they are challenged with not having the lifestyle they want. They want to solve this but they feel alone in finding a way to break away from work. The solution? Steve helps his clients design their life first and then systematize their business around that to reach millions of dollars in new revenue. As a result, they gain more business and more life.

Steve's *proven* marketing and sales systems have helped thousands of people grow their businesses, earn more money, and regain the personal freedom they want and choose. His *breakthrough* training and keynote speeches are *renown* for being simple, life-changing, and *fun*!

SteveNapolitan.com

Robyn Crane is a 4-time #1 Bestselling Author, Speaker, Coach, and Trainer. She is also host of the TV show, The Financial G-Spot and the radio show, Let's Talk Money. Her blueprint for financial and relationship success has been featured on Fox Business News, The Motley Fool and SavingsAccount.com. Her mission is to help people make more money, so they can help more people.

For over 10 years, Robyn's proven process has helped thousands of people succeed even if they feel horrible, unworthy, undeserving, and inadequate. Her secret success phenomenon is transforming lives like wildfire; female entrepreneurs can literally "feel they suck," but succeed anyway.

RobynCrane.com

Trevor Crane is a 10-time #1 international bestselling author, speaker, and the founder of Epic Author Publishing.

Trevor works with business owners, speakers, coaches and consultants who have the challenge of getting leads and elevating their brand. He helps them become irresistible to their ideal target client, while consistently growing their leads, sales and revenue.

Trevor's mission is to help people take their life and their businesses to the next level—no matter how successful they already are.

He is also the co-founder of, Super Kids Books Publishing, which he runs with his 10-year old daughter, Phoenix Rose Crane. She is also an author and has published NINE #1 international bestsellers. She's on a mission to help 1,000 kids become kids books authors.

"There is a proven path to go from blank page to bestseller in 90-days or less. You can write a great book fast and turn it into your most powerful marketing tool."
—Trevor Crane

TrevorCrane.com

1hour6figures.com/bonus

www.ingramcontent.com/pod-product-compliance
Lightning Source LLC
Chambersburg PA
CBHW071423180526
45170CB00001B/207